STRESS MANAG

CW00507791

ALLEVIATE TO MITIGATE

Raise Yourself Above The Threshold For Happiness and Peace

Kurt Long

Table of Contents

Chapter 1:

Why You Are Amazing

When was the last time you told yourself that you were amazing? Was it last week, last month, last year, or maybe not even once in your life?

As humans, we always seek to gain validation from our peers. We wait to see if something that we did recently warranted praise or commendation. Either from our colleagues, our bosses, our friends, or even our families. And when we don't receive those words that we expect them to, we think that we are unworthy, or that our work just wasn't good enough. That we are lousy and under serving of praise.

With social media and the power of the internet, these feelings have been amplified. For those of us that look at the likes on our Instagram posts or stories, or the number of followers on Tiktok, Facebook, or Snapchat, we allow ourselves to be subjected to the validation of external forces in order to qualify our self-worth. Whether these are strangers who don't know you at all, or whoever they might be, their approval seems to matter the most to us rather than the approval we can choose to give ourselves.

We believe that we always have to up our game in order to seek happiness. Everytime we don't get the likes, we let it affect our mood for the rest of the day or even the week.

Have you ever thought of how wonderful it is if you are your best cheerleader in life? If the only validation you needed to seek was from yourself? That you were proud of the work you put out there, even if the world disagrees, because you know that you have put your heart and soul into the project and that there was nothing else you could have done better in that moment when you were producing that thing?

I am here to tell you that you are amazing because only you have the power to choose to love yourself unconditionally. You have the power to tell yourself that you are amazing. and that you have the power to look into yourself and be proud of how far you came in life. To be amazed by the things that you have done up until this point, things that other people might not have seen, acknowledged, or given credit to you for. But you can give that credit to yourself. To pat yourself on the back and say "I did a great job".

I believe that we all have this ability to look inwards. That we don't need external forces to tell us we are amazing because deep down, we already know we are.

If nobody else in the world loves you, know that I do. I love your courage, your bravery, your resilience, your heart, your soul, your commitment, and your dedication to live out your best life on this earth. Tell yourself each and everyday that you deserve to be loved, and that you are loved.

Go through life fiercely knowing that you don't need to seek happiness, validations, and approval from others. That you have it inside you all along and that is all you need to keep going.

Chapter 2:

5 Ways To Deal with Personal Feelings of Inferiority

Have you at some point felt that you are inferior to others? That's normal. All of us, at some point in our lives, have felt the same. Growing up, we saw other kids who performed better than us in the class. Kids who played sports well. Kids who were loved by all. We got jealous. We felt inferior to them. We constantly compared ourselves to them.

Almost everyone has experienced that in their childhood. But do you still feel the same about others? Do you constantly analyze situations and people around you? Do you feel worthless? Then you probably have an inferiority complex. But the good news is you can get over this inferiority complex. We are going to list some of the things that will help you in doing that.

1. Build self-confidence

Treat yourself better. Act confident. Do what you love. Embrace yourself. Is there anything in your body that you don't feel confident about? Maybe your smile, your nose, or your hair? The trick here is to either accept yourself the way you are or do something about it. If you have curly hair, get your hair straightener. Do whatever makes you feel better about yourself.

2. Surround yourself with people who uplift you

It's important to realize that your inferiority complex might be linked to the people around you. It might be your relatives, your friends at college, your siblings, or your colleagues. Analyze your interactions with them.

Once you can identify people who try to pull you down, do not reciprocate your feelings, or are not very encouraging, start distancing yourself from them. Look for positive people, who uplift you, and who bring out the better version of yourself. Take efforts to develop a relationship with them.

3. Stop worrying about what other people think.

One major cause of inferiority complexes is constantly thinking about what others are thinking about us. We seek validation from them for every action of ours. Sometimes we are thinking about their actions, while sometimes, we imagine what they think.

4. Stop worrying about what other people think.

One major cause of inferiority complexes is constantly thinking about what others are thinking about us. We seek validation from them for every action of ours. Sometimes we are thinking about their actions, while sometimes, we are imagining what they think.

Disassociate yourself from their judgments. It's ultimately your opinion about yourself that matters. When we feel good about ourselves, others feel good about ourselves.

5. Do not be harsh on yourself.

There is no need to be harsh on yourself. Practice self-care. Love yourself. Be kind to yourself. Do not over-analyze situations. Do not expect yourself to change overnight. Give yourself time to heal.

Chapter 3:

How To Worry Less

How many of you worry about little things that affect the way you go about your day? That when you're out with your friends having a good time or just carrying out your daily activities, when out of nowhere a sudden burst of sadness enters your heart and mind and immediately you start to think about the worries and troubles you are facing. It is like you're fighting to stay positive and just enjoy your day but your mind just won't let you. It becomes a tug of war or a battle to see who wins?

How many of you also lose sleep because your mind starts racing at bedtime and you're flooded with sad feelings of uncertainty, despair, worthlessness or other negative emotions that when you wake up, that feeling of dread immediately overwhelms you and you just feel like life is too difficult and you just dont want to get out of bed.

Well If you have felt those things or are feeling those things right now, I want to tell you you're not alone. Because I too struggle with those feelings or emotions on a regular basis.

At the time of writing this, I was faced with many uncertainties in life. My business had just ran into some problems, my stocks weren't doing well, I had lost money, my bank account was telling me I wasn't good enough, but most importantly, i had lost confidence. I had lost the ability to face each day with confidence that things will get better. I felt that i was worthless and that bad things will always happen to me. I kept seeing the negative side of things and it took a great deal of emotional toll on me. It wasn't like i chose to think and feel these things, but they just came into my mind whenever they liked. It was like a parasite feeding off my negative energy and thriving on it, and weakening me at the same time.

Now your struggles may be different. You may have a totally different set of circumstances and struggles that you're facing, but the underlying issue is the same. We all go through times of despair, worry, frustration, and uncertainty. And it's totally normal and we shouldn't feel ashamed of it but to accept that it is a part of life and part of our reality.

But there are things we can do to minimise these worries and to shift to a healthier thought pattern that increases our ability to fight off these negative emotions.

I want to give you 5 actionable steps that you can take to worry less and be happier. And these steps are interlinked that can be carried out in fluid succession for the greatest benefit to you. But of course you can choose whichever ones speaks the most to you and it is more important that you are able to practice any one of these steps consistently rather than doing all 5 of them haphazardly. But I want to make sure I give you all the tools so that you can make the best decisions for yourself.

Try this with me right now as I go through these 5 steps and experience the benefit for yourself instead of waiting until something bad happens.

The very first step is simple. Just breathe. When a terrible feeling of sadness rushes into your body out of nowhere, take that as a cue to close your eyes, stop whatever you are doing, and take 5 deep breathes through your nose. Breathing into your chest and diaphragm. Deep breathing has the physiological benefit of calming your nerves and releasing tension in the body and it is a quick way to block out your negative thoughts. Pause the video if you need to do practice your deep breathing before we move on.

And as you deep breathe, begin the second step. Which is to practice gratefulness. Be grateful for what you already have instead of what you think u need to have to be happy. You could be grateful for your dog, your family, your friends, and whatever means the most to you. And if you cannot think of anything to be grateful for, just be grateful that you are even alive and walking on this earth today because that is special and amazing in its own right.

Next is to practice love and kindness to yourself. You are too special and too important to be so cruel to yourself. You deserve to be loved and you owe it to yourself to be kind and forgiving. Life is tough as it is, don't make it harder. If you don't believe in yourself, I believe in you and I believe in your worthiness as a person that you have a lot left to give.

The fourth step is to Live Everyday as if it were your last. Ask yourself, will you still want to spend your time worrying about things out of your control if it was your last day on earth? Will you be able to forgive yourself if you spent 23 out of the last 24 hours of your life worrying? Or will you choose to make the most out of the day by doing things that are meaningful and to practice love to your family, friends, and yourself?

Finally, I just want you to believe in yourself and Have hope that whatever actions you are taking now will bear fruition in the future. That they will not be in vain. That at the end of the day, you have done everything to the very best of your ability and you will have no regrets and you have left no stone unturned.

How do you feel now? Do you feel that it has helped at least a little or even a lot in shaping how you view things now? That you can shift your perspective and focus on the positives instead of the worries?

If it has worked for you today, I want to challenge you to consistently practice as many of these 5 steps throughout your daily lives every single day. When you feel a deep sadness coming over you, come back to this video if you need guidance, or practice these steps if you remember them on your own.

Chapter 4:

Motivation With Good Feelings

Ever wonder what goes on in your mind when you feel depressed isn't always the reaction to the things that happen to you? What you go through when you feel down is the chemistry of your brain that you yourself allow being created in the first place.

You don't feel weak just because your heart feels so heavy. You feel weak because you have filled your heart with all these feelings that don't let you do something useful.

Feelings are not your enemy till you choose the wrong ones. In fact, Feelings and emotions can be the strongest weapon to have in your arsenal.

People say, "You are a man, so act like one. Men don't cry, they act strong and brave"

You must make yourself strong enough to overcome any feelings of failure or fear. Any thought that makes you go aloof and dims that light of creativity and confidence. It's OK to feel sad and cry for some time, but it's not OK to feel weak for even a second.

Your consciousness dictates your feelings. Your senses help you to process a moment and in turn help you translate them into feelings that go both ways. This process has been going on from the day you were born and will continue till your last day.

You enter your consciousness as soon as you open your eyes to greet the day. It is at this moment when your creativity is at its peak. What you need now is just a set of useful thoughts and emotions that steer your whole day into a worthwhile one.

Don't spend your day regretting and repressing things you did or someone else did to you. You don't need these feelings right now. Because you successfully passed those tests of life and are alive still to be grateful for what you have right now.

There are a billion things in life to be thankful for and a billion more to be sad for. But you cannot live a happy fulfilling life if you focus on the later ones.

Life is too short to be sad and to be weak. When you start your day, don't worry about what needs to be done. But think about who you need to be to get those things done.

Don't let actions and outcomes drive you. Be the sailor of yourself to decide what outcomes you want.

Believe me, the feeling of gratitude is the biggest motivator. Self gratitude should be the level of appraisal to expect. Nothing should matter after your own opinions about yourself.

If you let other people's opinions affect your feelings, you are the weakest person out there. And failure is your destination.

Visualization of a better life can help you feel and hope better. It would help you to grow stronger and faster but remember; The day you lose control of your emotions, feelings, and your temper, your imagination will only lead you to a downward spiral.

Chapter 5:

ARE YOU PATIENT ENOUGH?

Think about it for a minute. We all want instant gratification and want things without waiting. We expect packages delivered the same day. We expect immediate results in the gym. We have food delivered to us already pre-cut to get a meal cooked 10 minutes faster. We can even have a book read to us or summarized so that we don't have to read them. I think that has to lead us to a life where we have very little patience. Maybe it is time we slow down and practice a little patience. Patience is also very important when you are a business owner. During your journey as a business owner, executive, or leader, you will have people say things about you that are unkind, unfair, and sometimes simply untrue. It happened to jesus and will happen to you! Here are four ways to be the patient person you never thought you could be.

1. Make yourself wait

The best way to practice patience is to make yourself wait. A study published in psychological science shows that waiting for things makes us happier in the long run. Start with something small like waiting a few extra minutes to drink that milkshake and then move on to something bigger. You will begin to gain more patience as you practice.

2. Stop doing things that aren't important

We all have things in our lives that take time away from what is important. One way of removing stress from our lives is to stop doing those things. Take a few minutes and evaluate your week. Look at your schedule from when you wake up to the time you go to sleep. Take out two or three things that you do that aren't important but take time. It's time to learn to say no to things that cause stress and make us impatient.

3. Be mindful of the things making you impatient

Most people have several tasks in their heads, and they jump from thought to thought without taking the time to finish one task first. We live interrupted lives as we try to multitask, and it is frustrating when we feel we aren't making progress. It is better to be mindful of our thoughts, and the best way to understand this is to write down what makes you impatient. This will help you slow down and focus on one task at a time and remove those things that stress you out.

4. Relax and take deep breaths

Most of all, just relax and take deep breaths. Taking slow deep breaths can help calm the mind and body. This is the easiest way to help ease any impatient feelings you are experiencing. If breathing doesn't help, i find taking a walk to clear your head can help you get refocused on what's important. The point is to find some time for you each day to decompress.

It is time we all slow down and practice a little more patience. We would be less stressed and more mindful of the things that stress us out. If that leads to being happier, then isn't it worth trying?

Chapter 6:

Happy People are Okay with Not Being Okay

All of us have a tendency where we constantly try to make people feel better about ourselves. We are fundamentally driven by empathy and compassion but what happens often is that these two are misdirected. Then we put our idea of okay onto other people and ourselves. Have you ever wondered what would it feel like when we simply whatever comes our way? When we are physically sick, of course, we take medicines to feel better, but there are also times when we are in emotional pain, and then we have no medicine to take and what happens is we seek out a solution, and that puts off the process where we can feel our feelings.

If you go through a breakup and do not allow yourself to feel the pain, what you will do is harm the next person you will date or sabotage your relationship with them. What will heal your wound is actively processing your emotions. This is not at all going to be comfortable, but it is essential for your emotional growth. What you need to do is start shedding the shame that surrounds not being okay. Just because you are in pain and not at the top of your work does not mean that you are weak. You also need to know that you are not the only one who thinks like that. We have been conditioned in this way of dysfunctional thinking and feeling. Most of us think that this is normal and normal is fine, but if you talk about health, that is a different story.

Of course, there are actions that you take that help you release the emotional pain you are in, but you have to remember that almost all of these actions will ask you to focus on yourself before you start focusing on others—for example, yoga. Yoga teaches you that your pain is not permanent, and it also tells us about how we have to be in an uncomfortable pose for a while to release that pain.

You have to remember that the only focus over here is you and you alone, but because we are all on a journey, we do get wind up in others' problems, which helps us find profound connections with them. It is okay to feel scared, or to feel pain, to feel uncertain, to feel lonely, to feel grief, it is okay to not be okay, and these are some of the things that you should never forget.

All the pain that you are feeling right now is not permanent. It will eventually pass. What you can do is honour your emotional experience by not avoiding it and being present for it; you should not try to distract yourself with every fibre of your being. This is a process that will help you heal and grow and move forward on this road. Show up for whatever you feel, even if it is just for a day.

Chapter 7:

How to Face Difficulties in Life

Have you noticed that difficulties in life come in gangs attacking you when you're least prepared for them? The effect is like being forced to endure an unrelenting nuclear attack.

Overcoming obstacles in life is hard. But life is full of personal challenges, and we have to summon the courage to face them. These test our emotional mettle — injury, illness, unemployment, grief, divorce, death, or even a new venture with an unknown future. Here are some strategies to help carry you through:

1. Turn Toward Reality

So often, we turn away from life rather than toward it. We are masters of avoidance! But if we want to be present—to enjoy life and be more effective in it—we must orient ourselves toward facing reality. When guided by the reality principle, we develop a deeper capacity to deal with life more effectively. What once was difficult is now easier. What once frightened us now feels familiar. Life becomes more manageable. And there's something even deeper that we gain: Because we can see that we have grown stronger, we have greater confidence that we can grow even stronger still. This is the basis of feeling capable, which is the wellspring of a satisfying life.

2. Embrace Your Life as It Is Rather Than as You Wish It to Be

The Buddha taught that the secret to life is to want what you have and do not want what you don't have. Being present means being present to the life that you have right here, right now. There is freedom in taking life as it comes to us—the good with the bad, the wonderful with the tragic, the love with the loss, and the life with the death. When we embrace it all, then we have a real chance to enjoy life, value our experiences, and mine the treasures that are there for the taking. When we surrender to the reality of who we are, we give ourselves a chance to do what we can do.

3. Take Your Time

As the story of the tortoise and the hare tells us, slow and steady wins the race. By being in a hurry, we actually thwart our own success. We get ahead of ourselves. We make more mistakes. We cut corners and pay for them later. We may learn the easy way but not necessarily the best way. As an old adage puts it: The slower you go, the sooner you get there. Slow, disciplined, incremental growth is the kind of approach that leads to lasting change.

Chapter 8:

Deal With Your Fears Now

Fear is a strange thing.

Most of our fears are phantoms that never actually appear or become real,

Yet it holds such power over us that it stops us from making steps forward in our lives.

It is important to deal with fear as it not only holds you back but also keeps you caged in irrational limitations.

Your life is formed by what you think.

It is important not to dwell or worry about anything negative.

Don't sweat the small stuff, and it's all small stuff (Richard Carlson).

It's a good attitude to have when avoiding fear.

Fear can be used as a motivator for yourself.

If you're in your 30s, you will be in your 80s in 50 years, then it will be too late.

And that doesn't mean you will even have 50 years. Anything could happen.

But let's say you do, that's 50 years to make it and enjoy it.

But to enjoy it while you are still likely to be healthy, you have a maximum of 15 years to make it - minus sleep and living you are down to 3 years.

If however you are in your 40s, you better get a move on quickly.

Does that fear not dwarf any possible fears you may have about taking action now?
Dealing with other fears becomes easy when the ticking clock is staring you in the face.
Most other fears are often irrational.

We are only born with two fears, the fear of falling and the fear of load noises.
The rest have been forced on us by environment or made up in our own minds.
The biggest percentage of fear never actually happens.

To overcome fear we must stare it in the face and walk through it knowing our success is at the other side.
Fear is a dream killer and often stops people from even trying.
Whenever you feel fear and think of quitting, imagine behind you is the ultimate fear of the clock ticking away your life.

If you stop you lose and the clock is a bigger monster than any fear.
If you let anything stop you the clock will catch you.

So stop letting these small phantoms prevent you from living,
They are stealing your seconds, minutes, hours , days and weeks.
If you carry on being scared, they will take your months, years and decades.

Before you know it they have stolen your life.

You are stronger than fear but you must display true strength that fear will be scared.
It will retreat from your path forever if you move in force towards it because fear is fear and by definition is scared.

We as humans are the scariest monsters on planet Earth.
So we should have nothing to fear
Fear tries to stop us from doing our life's work and that is unacceptable.
We must view life's fears as the imposters they are, mere illusions in our mind trying to control us.

We are in control here.
We have the free will to do it anyway despite fear.
Take control and fear will wither and disappear as if it was never here.
The control was always yours you just let fear steer you off your path.

Fear of failure, fear of success, fear of what people will think.
All irrational illusions.
All that matters is what you believe.
If your belief and faith in yourself is strong , fear will be no match for your will.

Les Brown describes fear as false evidence appearing real.
I've never seen a description so accurate.

Whenever fear rears its ugly head, just say to yourself this is false evidence appearing real.

Overcoming fear takes courage and strength in one's self.
We must develop more persistence than the resistance we will face when pursuing our dreams.
If we do not develop a thick skin and unwavering persistence we will be beaten by fear, loss and pain.

Our why must be so important that these imposters become small in comparison.
Because after all the life we want to live does dwarf any fears or set back that might be on the path.
Fear is insignificant.
Fear is just one thing of many we must beat into the ground to prove our worth.
Just another test that we must pass to gain our success.

Because success isn't your right,
You must fight
With all your grit and might
Make it through the night and shine your massive light on the world.
And show everyone you are a star.

Chapter 9:

Planning Ahead

The topic that are going to discuss today is probably one that is probably not going to apply to everybody, especially for those who have already settled down with a house, wife, kids, a stable career, and so on. But i still believe that we can all still learn something from it. And that is to think about planning ahead. Or rather, thinking long term.

You see, for the majority of us, we are trained to see maybe 1 to 2 years ahead in our lives. Being trained to do so in school, we tend to look towards our next grade, one year at a time. And this system has ingrained in us that we find it hard to see what might and could happen 2 or 3 years down the road.

Whilst there is nothing wrong with living life one year at a time, we tend to fall into a short term view of what we can achieve. We tell ourselves we must learn a new instrument within 1 year and be great at it, or we must get this job in one year and become the head of department, or we must find our partner and get married within a short amount of time. However, life does not really work that way, and things actually do take much longer, and we do actually need more time to grow these small little shoots into big trees.

We fail to see that we might have to give ourselves a longer runway time of maybe 3-5 or even 10 years before we can become masters in a new instrument, job, relationship, or even friendships. Rome isn't built in a day and we shouldn't expect to see results if we only allow ourselves 1 year to accomplish those tasks. Giving ourselves only 1 year to achieve the things we want can put unnecessary pressure on ourselves to expect results fast, when in reality no matter how much you think u think rushing can help you achieve results faster, you might end up burning yourself out instead.

For those short term planners, even myself. I have felt that at many stages in my life, i struggle to see the big picture. I struggle to see how much i can achieve in lets say 5 years if i only allowed myself that amount of time to become a master in whatever challenge i decide to take on. Even the greatest athletes take a longer term view to their career. They believe that if they practice hard each day, they might not expect to see results in the first year, but as their efforts compound, by the 5th year they would have already done so much practice that it is statistically impossible not to be good at it.

And when many of us fall into the trap of simply planning short term, our body reacts by trying to rush the process as well. We expect everything to be fast fast fast, and results to be now now now. And we set unrealistic goals that we cannot achieve and we beat ourselves up for it come December 31st.

Instead i believe many of us should plan ahead by giving ourselves a minimum of 2.5 years in whatever task we set to achieve, be it an income goal, a fitness goal, or a relationship goal. 2.5 years is definitely much more manageable and it gives us enough room to breathe so that we don't stress ourselves out unnecessarily. If you feel like being kinder to yourself, you might even give yourselves up to 5 years.

And again the key to achieving success with proper long term planning is Consistency. If you haven't watched my video on consistency do check it out as i believe it is one of the most important videos that I have ever created.

I believe that with a run time of 5 years and consistency in putting the hours every single day, whether it is an hour or 10 hours, that by the end of it, there is no goal that you cannot achieve. And we should play an even longer game of 10 years or so. Because many of the changes we want to make in life should be permanent and sustainable. Not a one off thing.

So I challenge each and everyone of you today to not only plan ahead, but to think ahead of the longevity of the path that you have set for yourself. There is no point rushing through life and missing all the incredible sights along the way. I am sure you will be a much happier person for it.

Chapter 10:

Happy People Have A Morning Ritual

For many of us, mornings begin in a rushed panic. We allow our alarm clocks to buzz at least a dozen times before deciding we have to get out of bed. Then we rush around our homes half-awake, trying to get ready for our day. In a hurry, we stub our toe on the bedpost, forget to put on deodorant, and don't pack a lunch because we simply don't have time. It's no wonder that so many folks despise the thought of being awake before 9 a.m.!

So it may not surprise you to know that the happiest and healthiest people tend to enjoy their mornings. They appear to thrive on waking up with the sun and look forward to a new day of possibilities. These people have humble morning rituals that increase their sense of well-being and give their day purpose.

Here are 3 morning habits that healthy and happy people tend to share:

1.   They wake up with a sense of gratitude

Practicing gratitude is associated with a sense of overall happiness and a better mood—so it makes sense that the happiest and healthiest people we know start the day with a gratitude practice. This means that they're truly appreciative of their life and all of its little treasures. They practice small acts of gratitude in the morning by expressing thankfulness to their partner each morning before they rise from bed. They may also write about their gratefulness for five minutes each morning in a journal that they keep by their bedside.

2. They begin every morning anew.

The happiest and healthiest people know that every day is a brand-new day—a chance to start over and do something different. Yesterday may have been a complete failure for them, but today is a new day for success and adventure. Individuals who aren't ruined by one bad day are resilient creatures. Resiliency is a telltale sign of having purpose and happiness.

3. They take part in affirmation, meditation, or prayer.

Many of the happiest folks alive are spiritual. Affirmations are a way of reminding ourselves of all that we have going for us, and they allow us to engrain in our minds the kind of person we wish to be. Meditation helps keep our mind focused, calms our nerves, and supports inner peace. If you're already spiritual, prayer is a great way to connect and give thanks for whatever higher power you believe in.

Chapter 11:

The Power of Imperfect Starts

When you have a goal — starting a business or eating healthier, or traveling the world — it's easy to look at someone who is already doing it and then try to reverse engineer their strategy. In some cases, this is useful. Learning from the experiences of successful people is a great way to accelerate your learning curve.

But it's equally important to remember that the systems, habits, and strategies that successful people are using today are probably not the same ones they were using when they began their journey. What is optimal for them right now isn't necessarily needed for you to get started. There is a difference between the two.

Let me explain.

What is Optimal vs. What is Needed

Learning from others is great, and I do it all the time myself.

But comparing your current situation to someone already successful can often make you feel like you lack the required resources to get started at all. If you look at their optimal setup, it can be really easy to convince yourself that you need to buy new things or learn new skills or meet new people before you can even take the first step toward your goals.

And usually, that's not true. Here are two examples.

Starting a business. When you're an entrepreneur, it's so easy to get obsessed with optimal. This is especially true at the start. I can remember being convinced that my first website would not succeed without a great logo. After all, every popular website I looked at had a professional logo. I've since learned my lesson. Now my "logo" is just my name, and this is the most popular website I've built.

Eating healthy. Maybe the optimal diet would involve buying beef that is only grass-fed or vegetables that are only organic, or some other super-healthy food strategy. But if you're just trying to make strides in the right direction, why get bogged down in the details? Start small and simply buy another vegetable this week — whether it's organic or not. There will be plenty of time for optimization later.

Avoiding by Optimizing

Claiming that you need to "learn more" or "get all of your ducks in a row" can often be a crutch that prevents you from moving forward on the stuff that matters.

- You can complain that your golf game is suffering because you need new clubs, but the truth is you probably just need two years of practice.

- You can point out how your business mentor is successful because they use XYZ software, but they probably got started without it.

Obsessing about the ultimate strategy, diet, or golf club can be a clever way to prevent yourself from doing hard work.

An imperfect start can always be improved, but obsessing over a perfect plan will never take you anywhere on its own.

Chapter 12:

Five Habits of A Healthy Lifestyle

A healthy lifestyle is everybody's dream. The young and old, rich and poor, weak and strong, and male and female all want a happily ever after and many years full of life. The price to pay to achieve this dream is what distinguishes all these classes of people. What are you ready to forego as the opportunity cost to have a healthy lifestyle?

Here are five habits for a healthy lifestyle.

1. Eating Healthy Food

Your health is heavily dependent on your diet. You have heard that what goes inside a man does not defile him, but what goes out of him does. In this case, the opposite is true. What a man takes as food or beverage affects him directly. It can alter the body's metabolism and introduce toxins in the body hence endangering his life.

Most people do not take care of what they feed on. They eat anything edible that is readily available without any consideration. All other factors like the nutritive value of the food and its hygiene are secondary to most modern people who have thrown caution to the wind. Towns and cities are full of fast food joints and attract masses from all over. It is the most lucrative business these days. Are these fast foods healthy?

As much as the hygiene could be up to standards (due to the measures put in place by authorities), the composition of these foods (mostly chips and broiler chicken) is wanting. The cooking oil used is full of cholesterol that is a major cause of cardiac diseases. To lead a healthy lifestyle, eating healthy food should be a priority.

2. Regular Exercising

The human body requires regular exercise to be fit. Running, walking, swimming, or going to the gym are a few of the many ways that people can exercise. It is a call to get out of your comfort zone to ward off some lifestyle diseases. It is often misconstrued that exercising is a reserve for sportsmen and women. This fallacy has taken root in the minds of many people.

Unlearn the myths about exercises that have made most people shun them. The benefits of exercising are uncountable. It improves pressure and blood circulation in the body. Exercises also burn excess calories in tissues that would otherwise clog blood vessels and pose a health hazard. Research has shown that most people who exercise are healthy and fall sick less often. This is everyone's dream but the few who choose to pay the price enjoy it. Choose to be healthy by doing away with frequent motor vehicle transport and instead walk. A simple walk is an exercise already. When you fail to exercise early enough, you will be a frequent patient at the hospital. Prevention is always better than cure.

In the words of world marathon champion, Eliud Kipchoge, a running nation is a healthy nation.

3. Regular Medical Checkup

When was the last time you went for a medical checkup even when you were not sick? If the answer is negative or a long time ago, then a healthy lifestyle is still unreachable. A medical examination will reveal any disease in its early stages.

In most third-world countries, healthcare systems are not fully developed. Its citizens only go to the hospital when a disease has progressed and is in its late stages. At such a time, there is a higher probability of the patient succumbing to it. Doctors advise people to seek medical attention at the slightest symptom to treat and manage long-term illnesses. Regular medical checkups help one become more productive at work.

Is a healthy lifestyle attainable? Yes, it is when one takes the necessary measures to fight diseases. Regular medical checkups can be financially draining. Seek an insurance policy that can underwrite your health risks and this will make medical expenses affordable.

4. Staying Positive

A bad attitude is like a flat tire. If you do not change it, you will never go anywhere. There is a hidden power in having a positive attitude towards life. It all starts in the mind. When you conceive the right attitude towards life, you have won half the battle.

A healthy lifestyle starts with the mind. If you believe it, you can achieve it. So limitless is the human mind that it strongly influences the direction of a person's life. As much as there are challenges in life, do not allow them to conquer your mind or take over your spirit. Once they do, you will be constantly waging a losing battle. Is that what we want?

Associate with positive like-minded people and you will be miles away from depression and low self-esteem. We all desire that healthy lifestyle.

5. Have A Confidant And A Best Friend

Who is a best friend? He/she is someone you can trust to share your joy and sadness, and your high and low moments. You should be careful in your selection of a confidant because it may have strong ramifications if the friendship is not genuine.

A confidant is someone you can confide in comfortably without fear of him/her leaking your secrets. He/she will help you overcome some difficult situations in life. We all need a shoulder to lean on in our darkest times and a voice to comfort us that it is darkest before dawn. This helps fortify our mental health. We grow better and stronger in this healthy lifestyle.

These are the five habits for a healthy lifestyle. When we live by them, success becomes our portion.

Chapter 13:

The Downside of Work-Life Balance

One way to think about work-life balance is with a concept known as The Four Burners Theory. Here's how it was first explained to me:

Imagine that a stove represents your life with four burners on it. Each burner symbolizes one major quadrant of your life.

1. The first burner represents your family.

2. The second burner is your friends.

3. The third burner is your health.

4. The fourth burner is your work.

The Four Burners Theory says that "to be successful, you have to cut off one of your burners. And to be successful, you have to cut off two."

The View of the Four Burners

My initial reaction to The Four Burners Theory was to search for a way to bypass it. "Can I succeed and keep all four burners running?" I wondered.

Perhaps I could combine two burners. "What if I lumped family and friends into one category?"

Maybe I could combine health and work. "I hear sitting all day is unhealthy. What if I got a standing desk?" Now, I know what you are thinking. Believing that you will be healthy because you bought a standing desk is like believing you are a rebel because you ignored the fasten seatbelt sign on an airplane, but whatever.

Soon I realized I was inventing these workarounds because I didn't want to face the real issue: life is filled with tradeoffs. If you want to excel in your work and your marriage, then your friends and your health may have to suffer. If you want to be healthy and succeed as a parent, then you might be forced to dial back your career ambitions. Of course, you are free to divide your time equally among all four burners, but you have to accept that you will never reach your full potential in any given area.

Essentially, we are forced to choose. Would you rather live a life that is unbalanced but high-performing in a certain area? Or would you rather live a life that is balanced but never maximizes your potential in a given quadrant?

Option 1: Outsource Burners

We outsource small aspects of our lives all the time. We buy fast food, so we don't have to cook. We go to the dry cleaners to save time on laundry. We visit the car repair shop, so we don't have to fix our automobile.

43

Outsourcing small portions of your life allow you to save time and spend it elsewhere. Can you apply the same idea to one quadrant of your life and free up time to focus on the other three burners?

Work is the best example. For many people, work is the hottest burner on the stove. It is where they spend the most time, and it is the last burner to get turned off. In theory, entrepreneurs and business owners can outsource the work burner. They do it by hiring employees.

The Four Burners Theory reveals a truth everyone must deal with: nobody likes being told they can't have it all, but everyone has constraints on their time and energy. Every choice has a cost.

Which burners have you cut off?

Chapter 14:

Trust The Process

Today we're going to talk about the power of having faith that things will work out for you even though you can't see the end in sight just yet. And why you need to simply trust in the process in all the things that you do.

Fear is something that we all have. We fear that if we quit our jobs to pursue our passions, that we may not be able to feed ourselves if our dreams do not work out. We fear that if we embark on a new business venture, that it might fail and we would have incurred financial and professional setbacks.

All this is borne out of the fear of the unknown. The truth is that we really do not know what can or will happen. We may try to imagine in our heads as much as we can, but we can never really know until we try and experienced it for ourselves.

The only way to overcome the fear of the unknown is to take small steps, one day at a time. We will, to the best of our ability, execute the plan that we have set for ourselves. And the rest we leave it up to the confidence that our actions will lead to results.

If problems arise, we deal with it there and then. We put out fires, we implement updated strategies, and we keep going. We keep going until we have exhausted all avenues. Until there is no more roads for us to travel, no more paths for us to create. That is the best thing that we can do.

If we constantly focus on the fear, we will never go anywhere. If we constantly worry about the future, we will never be happy with the present. If we dwell on our past failures, we will be a victim of our own shortcomings. We will not grow, we will not learn, we will not get better.

I challenge each and every one of you today to make the best out of every situation that you will face. Grab fear by the horns and toss them aside as if it were nothing. I believe in you and all that you can achieve.

Chapter 15:

Don't Fear Judgement

People often seem to get caught up in certain areas of their lives where they have a lot to offer but don't actually have the guts to be transparent about it. Let me make some sense.

We all have this ability to get distracted by things that have very little to do with our actions. But have a lot to do with what others will say about us.

You go through a rough patch in life and then you find the balance. We have things that have been going on in our lives from the beginning, but we still feel doubts about it.

The doubt is natural. But if the doubts are a result of the presence of other people around you, then you have a problem at your hand. This problem is the fear of judgment that everyone imposes on us in their own unique ways.

Humans have a tendency to get out of their ways and try certain things that aren't always normal. They may be normal for some, but for most people out there, it's just another eccentric doing something strange.

So what? What is so bad about being a little different? What is wrong with thinking a little out of the box? Why should your approach be bad if someone doesn't approve of it?

These questions should not make you feel confused. Rather should help you get a much clearer idea of what you want. These questions and their answers can help you find the right motivation. The motivation to do your thing no matter what the others around you say or see.

You are the best judge of your deeds. Because no one else saw your intentions when you started. No one else saw the circumstances that led you to these actions. No other person was in your head looking at and feeling those incidents that carved your present state. But you were always there and always will be.

No one cares what you are up to until you get to the stage of being noticeable. People pass judgments because now you have made it into some sort of limelight. It may be your workplace, your college, or even a party where most people are stoned.

But think about it, what harm can you get with a couple of remarks about your outfit or an achievement?

The words that strike your ears and make you feel incompetent or stupid are just the insecurities of the people around you. The glare of shaming or mockery is only the reflection of the feeling that they don't have what you have.

So be who you are, and say what you want, and do what you feel. Because the people who mind don't matter. But the people who matter would never mind.

Come to terms with yourself and be confident with what you want to do or are currently up to.

No one would understand your reasons and no one is meant to. But they can make a judgment when you are finally on that rostrum. Then you'd have the power to shut anyone at any time.

Chapter 16:

How To Achieve True Happiness

How many of us actually know what happiness really is? And how many of us spend our whole lives searching for it but never seem to be happy?

I want to share with you my story today of how i stumbled upon true happiness and how you can achieve the same for yourself in your life.

Many of us go through the motion of trying to earn money because we think the more money we have, the better our lives will be. We chase the dream of increasing our earning power so that we can afford to buy nicer and more expensive things. And we believe that when we have more money, our happiness level will increase as well and we will be filled with so much money and happiness that we can finally stop chasing it.

Now I just wanna say, Yes, for those who come from a not so affluent background where they have a family to feed and basic needs have to be met to in order for them to survive, having a monetary goal to work towards is truly commendable as their drive, motivation, and sole purpose comes from supporting their family. Their sense of achievement, joy, and happiness comes from seeing their loved ones attaining basic needs and then go on to achieve success later in life at the expense of their time and energy. But they are more than okay with that and they do so with a willing heart, mind, and soul. You might even say that these people have achieved true happiness. Not because they are chasing more money, but because they are using that money to serve a greater purpose other than themselves.

But what about the rest of us who seemingly have everything we could ever want but never seem to be happy? We work hard at our jobs every single day waiting for our next promotion so that we can command a higher pay. And as our income grows, so does our appetite and desire for more expensive material things.

For guys we might chase that fancy new watch like rolex, omega, breitling, drooling over that model that always seem to be on a never-ending waitlist. And as we purchased one, feeling that temporary joy and satisfaction, we quickly look towards that next model as the shiny object we have starts to slowly fade. We lose our so-called happiness in time and We go back to work dreaming about that next watch just to feel that joy and excitement again. This could apply to other material things such as a shiny new technology gadgets smartphones, tv, and even cars.

For women, while might not be true for everyone, They might look towards that designer shoe, that branded handbag, ar that fancy jewellery that costs thousands of dollars to purchase but happily pay for it because they think it makes them feel better about ourselves. Or they could even use these purchases as retail therapy from their stressful lives and jobs.

Whatever these expensive purchases may be, we think that by spend our hard earned money on material things, it will bring us happiness and joy, but somehow it never does, and in most cases it is only temporary satisfactions.

That was exactly what happened with me. I kept chasing a higher income thinking it would bring me happiness. As a lover of technology, I always sought to buy the latest gadgets I could get my hands on. The excitement peaks and then fades. For me I realised that I had created an endless loop of trying to chase happiness but always coming up short.

One day I sat down and reflected on what exactly made me REALLY happy and I started writing down a list. My List Came down to these in no particular order: Spending time with family, spending time with friends, helping others, having a purpose in life, being at peace with myself, working on my own dreams, singing and making music, exercising, being grateful, and finally being a loving person to others.

As I went through this list, I realised that hey, in none of the list did i write "making more money" or "buying more things". And it finally dawned on me that these are REALLY the things that made me truly happy. And only after I had defined these things did i actively choose to do more of them every single day.

I started spending more quality time with my friends and family, i started playing my favourite sport (Tennis) a few times a week, I chose to be grateful that I can even be alive on this earth, and I chose to be more loving and humble. Finally I also actively chose not to compare myself to people who were more "successful" than I was because comparing yourself to others can NEVER make you happy and will only make you feel inferior when you are not. Always remember that You are special, you are unique, and you are amazing.

After doing these things every single day, I had become a much happier person. It is all about perspective.

So what can you do to achieve happiness for yourself?

I recommend that you do the same thing I did which is to write down a list under the title "When Am I The Happiest?" or "When Was A Time When I Truly Felt Happy?" Start breaking down these memories as you recall your past, and down the essence of the memory. Everybody's list will be different as happiness means different things to every one of us. Once you have your answer, start doing more of these things everyday and tell me how you feel afterwards.

Some days you will forget about what makes you truly happy as you get bombarded by the harsh and cruel things life will throw at you. So I encourage you to put this list somewhere visible where you can see it everyday. Constantly remind yourself of what happiness means to you and shift your mind and body towards these actions every single day. I am sure you will be much happier person after that.

Chapter 17:

Are You Trying Too Hard To Be A Perfectionist?

There's a fine line between having an achieving behavior and having a perfectionistic behavior. High achievers can be defined as determined, dedicated individuals who have a strong desire to accomplish important things. On the other hand, perfectionism has a flawed mindset that is driven by the avoidance of failure. True perfectionists don't try to be perfect but rather avoid not being good enough. This avoidance may dictate their behavior, leading to depression, anxiety, eating disorders, and even suicide.

Do you ever find yourself in a loop where you are scared of messing up even the tiniest of things? You keep obsessing over that essay over and over again to get it perfect, or you keep panicking over that outfit to get it right. Perfectionism manifests in many aspects of one's life. The stress of not being prepared or something not working out exactly as planned is perfectionism behavior.

Sure, this process may lead you to your desired outcome, like getting an A on that essay or causing someone in the hall to look twice at you. But the question remains, at what cost? How much did you stress over the smallest aspect of what you were trying to achieve? Was it the success that motivated you, or was it the fear of failure? And most importantly, are you being too hard on yourself?

The answer to all of the above questions is probably yes. We dive into everything so deeply that we forget there is no such thing as a perfect person. We are all full of flaws and mistakes. But still, we tend to strive for perfection, and we are looking to do things perfectly. And when it doesn't work out, it becomes detrimental to our progress and mental health. It would seem rather strange, but it is true that perfectionism can trigger procrastination, as the paralyzing fear that you will fail can stop you in your tracks. It's either if I can't do something perfectly, I shouldn't do it at all, or I have to wait for the perfect time to do this perfectly. This attitude would stop you from trying new things, putting yourself out there, or starting your tasks.

Being hard on yourself for trying to be perfect will worsen your mental health and affect your physical health. The blind pursuit of success can lead to neglect of your health and relationships. Recognize that no matter what the result will be, you have worked hard on your end. Acknowledge the efforts that you've put in reaching your goals. The work you do in achieving your goals is sometimes more important than the achievement itself. Find joy in setting goals rather than being weighed down by obligations.

Most importantly, get over it. Nobody's perfect, and you're no exception. Learn to accept your mistakes and flaws instead of holding yourself accountable for every shortcoming and keeping up your standards impossibly high.

Perfectionism is itself an imperfect way to look at life. Failing isn't the end of the world; and rather, it's the beginning of your success. You shouldn't let it get to you and stop you from pursuing your goals. Learn from the experiences and be kinder to yourself. You deserve it!

Chapter 18:

10 Habits of Steve Jobs

Steven Paul Jobs was an American innovator, designer, and undoubtedly successful businessman. He is a narrative of entrepreneurial creation myth: he transformed imagination into technology and entrepreneur skills. He helped usher in an era of personal and tablet computing, smartphones, animated films, music, digital publishing, and retail outlets. Steve founder Apple in his parents' garage in 1976 was ousted in 1985, but later returned to the company to save it when it was a purge of bankruptcy; by the time of his death in 2011, he transformed it into the world's most valuable company. Even if Steve is no longer here, his legacy will live on.

Here are 10 Steve Jobs habits that are worth your attention.

1. You Can Anticipate the Future

Steve Jobs is still a living example of someone who can predict future trends. His efforts have benefited Apple, as evidenced by the company's dominance in digital sales. The iPhone has transformed the phone market by introducing a very sophisticated touch-screen phone. One way to incorporate this into your life is by imagining yourself in years to come because having a vision will help you anticipate, prepare for hurdles and overcome them.

2. Don't Let Circumstances Limit Your Life.

Master a habit of seeing the positive in every situation and creating a channel to reap its benefits. As an adoptive child, Steve may easily have despised his upbringing or perhaps indulged in undesirable activities as a teenager. Instead, Steve focused on the good; he decided to devote his efforts to technology and computing, and you know how wonderfully that turned out.

3. Find the Ideal Partner

Apple was co-founded by Steve and his partner Steve Wozniak, who greatly complemented Job's skill set. Similarly, to be successful, you must choose the ideal companion in your life. The people you surround yourself with have the power to make or break your life.

4. Don't Sell Crap

While many would argue that Apple only sells high-quality products, you can agree that the quality is the reason why they are still at the top. It is simply through the provision of high-quality products that they have devoted clients who are constantly eager to purchase.

5. Obstacles Are Masked Opportunities

Once you learn to see obstacles as hidden opportunities, you'll always find a way to get away out. During the development of the first Apple computer, Jobs and Wozniak ran out of money. Instead of surrendering, Jobs sold his van, while Wozniak sold his graphing calculator. There is always a way when there is a will.

6. Take That Risk

Steve was willing to give up his company's products for the sake of advancement. Many CEOs would have been hesitant to develop an iPhone, knowing that it would almost certainly lead to the collapse of the iPod-but Jobs did it nonetheless. To progress, you must risk it. However, to make an informed decision, assess the risk's best and worst-case scenarios.

7. To Sell Your Idea, First Assess Whether it's Fit.

Compared to other companies, one thing unique about Steve and Apple is that Apple surprises the world with a new product that you could never have imagined. That is an example of empathy. That is seeing the world as it should be rather than as it is.

8. Redefine the Game

Rather than focusing on beating your competitors, redefine your game. Apple Inc. went from being on the verge of bankruptcy to releasing the iPhone ten years later because Steve played a computer game that other competitors didn't. While other smartphones featured physical keyboards, Apple developed touch-screen smartphones that most users preferred.

9. Explore the World and Try New Things

As an entrepreneur, traveling opens new windows and avenues. You must understand people from different places to instigate a consumerist understanding. After traveling to Ashram, India, Steve noted how it opened his mind to new market ideas in an interview.

10. Learning as a Child

According to Steve Jobs, learning is a continuous habit and an essential skill of success. Each time you learn a new thing, it reshapes your brain and enhances your focus. Consider how children approach learning in different ways. To them, it's merely a component of the exploration they utilize to confront the world around them.

Conclusion

Just like Steve Jobs, it all comes down to the initial step. If you have an idea, put it into action. It will die out if you do not start. Believe in your vision and get started.

Chapter 19:

The Struggle With Time

Today we're going to talk about a topic that isn't commonly looked at in depth. But it is one that we might hopefully find a new appreciation for. And that is TIME.

Time is a funny thing, we are never really aware of it and how much of a limited resource it really is until we get a rude awakening. Most commonly when our mortality is tested. Whether it be a health scare, an accident, a death of a loved one, a death of a pet, we always think we have more time before that. That we will always have time to say i love you, to put off the things we always told ourselves we needed to do, to start making that change, to spend time with the people that mean the most to us.

As we go about our days, weeks and months, being bothered and distracted by petty work, by our bosses, colleagues, trying to climb the corporate ladder, we forget to stop and check in on our fiends and family... We forget that their time may be running out, and that we may not have as much time with them as we think we do, until it is too late, and then we regret not prioritising them first. All the money that we made could not ever buy back the time we have lost with them. And that is something we have to live with if we ever let that happen.

The other funny thing about time is that if we don't set it aside for specific tasks, if we don't schedule anything, we will end up wasting it on something mindless. Whether it be browsing social media endlessly, or bingeing on television, we will never run out of things to fill that time with. Can you imagine that even though time is so precious, we willingly sacrifice and trade it in for self isolation in front of our TVs and computers for hours on end. Sometimes even for days? Or even on mobile games. Some being so addictive that it consumes most of our waking hours if we are not careful.

Our devices have become dangerous time wasters. It is a tool Shea its literally sapping the living energy out of us. Which is why some responsible companies have started implementing new features that help us keep track of our screen time. To keep us in check, and to not let our children get sucked into this black hole that we might struggle to climb out of.

I believe the biggest struggle with time that we all have is how to spend it in such a way that we can be happy without feeling guilty. Guilty of not spending it wisely. And I believe the best way to start is to start defining the things that you need to do, and the things that you want to do. And then striking a balance. To set equal amounts of time into each activity so that it doesn't overwhelm or underwhelm you. Spend one hour on each activity each day that you feel will have an impact on your life in a meaningful way, and you can spend your time on television or games without remorse.

So I challenge each of you to make the most of your time. SPending time with loved ones always come first, followed by your goals and dreams, and then leisure activities. Never the other way around. That way you can be at the end of your life knowing that you had not wasted the most precious commodity that we are only given a finite amount of. Money can't buy back your youth, your health, or time with loved ones, so don't waste it.

Chapter 20:

7 Ways On How To Attract Success In Life

Successful people fail more times than unsuccessful people try. A new thought author and metaphysical writer Florence Scovel Shinn in her timeless 1940 novel, 'the secret door to success,' suggests that "Success is not a secret, it is a system." Throughout the centuries, the leaders have alluded to the possibility that success can be attracted into one's life simply by thinking and doing. It is rather a planned journey as we give validity to the premise of creating a plan or setting a goal for ourselves. Goals are set to be achieved, and achievements pave the way for success. Here are 7 Ways To Attract Success In Your Life:

1. Define What Success Means To You

Success is subjective to the person who seeks to obtain it, and the ideas may be different for each other. For some of us, success means wealth. For some, it means health and happiness. While for some, it is the mere effort of getting out of bed every day. But the thing that is most highlighted is that we can never get success without struggling. Every one of us wants success, but we do not know how to bring about that life-changing phenomenon that will take us to the zenith of our potential.

2. Begin with Gratitude:

From flying to the sky to crashing to the ground, be always thankful to wherever life takes you. Always start by being grateful for what you already have. Whether it's good or bad, we cannot climb the stairs of success without having experiences. If we make mistakes, we should make sure not to give up, rather learn from those mistakes. We must strive to embrace our flaws and imperfections. If we tend to fall seven times, we must have the energy to get up eight times. Whatever life throws us at, no matter the obstacles and challenges, we should always be in a state of gratitude and always be thankful for our learning.

3. Stop making excuses:

Your decisions lead to your destiny. If you are thinking about delaying your work or 'chilling' first, then someone else will take that opportunity for himself. You either grab on the opportunities from both hands, or you sit on the sidelines and watch someone else steal your spotlight. There's no concept of resting and being lazy when you have to work towards your goals and achieve your dreams. One of the major mistakes of unsuccessful people is that they make endless excuses. They would avoid their tasks in any way instead of working on them and actually doing them. You will attract success only if you put your mind towards something and work hard towards it.

4. Realize your potential:

The fine line between incredibly hardworking people and yet fail to achieve success, and the ones who are at the peak of their respective field is simple – potential. We never realize our true potential until we are put in a situation where there's no way out but to express our abilities. We might think that people have more excellent skills than us or have more knowledge than us. But the truth is, we have more potential inside of us. This might be tougher to implement as we don't know how well we can handle things while stressing out or how much hidden talents and skills we possess. Our potential is merely what might make us successful or a failure. It all depends on how much we are willing to try and push ourselves forward.

5. Celebrate the success of others:

What you wish upon others finds its way and comes back to you again. While seeing people being successful in their professional and personal lives and making a fortune in their careers and businesses can be tough on our lives, always remember that they too faced struggles and challenges before reaching here. There's no need to be envious as life has an abundance of everything to offer to everyone. Whatever is it in your destiny will always find its way to you. You can't snatch what others have achieved, and similarly, others can't seize whatever that you have or may achieve. Congratulate people around you and be excited for them. Send out positive vibes to everyone so you may receive the same.

6. Behave as if you are successful:

Have you heard of the term "fake it till you make it?" Well, it applies to this scenario too. You can fake your success and act like a successful person until you really become one. First, surround yourself with lucrative people. See what habits they have developed over time, how they dress up, how they behave, and, most importantly, how much work they do daily to achieve their goals. Get inspired from them and adopt their healthy habits. Be successful in your own eyes first so that eventually you can be successful in other's eyes as well.

7. Provide value for others:

While money and fame are the most common success goals, we should first try to focus on creating value in the world. A lot of successful people wanted to change things in the world first and help people out. Mark Zuckerberg built a tool for Harvard students initially and now has over 1.4 billion users. The first thing on our mind after waking up shouldn't be money or success, and it would be to create value for the world and the people around us.

Conclusion:

It would be best if you strived to explore the unique, endless possibilities within you. Then, when you start working on yourself, you're adding to your mind's youth, vitality, and beauty.

Chapter 21:

The Magic of the 5 Minute Rule

Recently I have been struggling to get things done, more so than usual. It has become a daily battle with myself to sit down on my desk to begin the necessary work that I know i need to do. However looking at the endless list of tasks i have in front of me, i can't help but to choose procrastination and slacking over beginning my work. And it has affected my ability to be a productive member of society.

Whilst I knew in the back of my mind that I believe the work that I do can benefit society, and that it has the power to give me freedom of time and money to get and do the things that i really wanted to do in life, on some level it wasn't actually enough to get me to start the work. Many a times I felt really sluggish and it would take some strong reminders to get me motivated enough to start the work. That was the point where i decided i needed to search for a solution that work not only make work more enjoyable, but to also push me to get work started much faster without delay.

After spending some solid hours researching, i came across one strategy that I felt would work like a charm on me. And that is to employ the 5 minute rule to every single task that I have on hand.

The biggest problem that I have currently is that I am working on 10 different projects at any one time. And when I look at these 10 separate projects that need my attention, I can't help but feel overwhelmed about the number of hours that I needed to schedule for each of these projects. And that seemed like a mountainous task for me to climb. And looking at it as a whole, it felt absolutely daunting and impossible. Which was what made me not want to even attempt to begin that climb.

How the 5 minute rule works is that for every project that I needed to work on, I wrote that I only needed to do the task for 5 minutes. However ridiculous that sounded, it actually worked like a charm. My brain was tricked into thinking that this became much more manageable and i would accomplish it easily. And we all know that the biggest problem is getting started. But once u do, you tend to keep going. And so for every task that i told myself i needed to do for 5 minutes, in reality i ended up spending the adequate amount of time i needed to do to get the job done. whether it be 10 minutes, 30minutes, an hour, or even several hours.

I managed to trick my brain into breaking each project down to its most basic manageable form and that gave me to confidence that I could crush it with ease. I applied this technique to not only work, but also going to the gym, walking my dog, and other administrative and personal tasks that I was lazy to do. And i saw my ability to begin each task and eventually check it off my to-do list increase exponentially. My productivity level also skyrocketed as a result.

With this simple trick in your arsenal. I believe anyone that you too can begin your work much quicker as well and crush every single task that will be put in front of you today and in your future. So i challenge each and everyone of you today to just tell yourself that you will only need to set aside 5 mins for each task and see where that takes you, and that I believe will be in the right direction.

Chapter 22:

Avoid The Dreaded Burnout

Do you often lack the energy to get on with any new task and feel sluggish throughout most of your day? Do you feel the burden of work that keeps getting pilled up each day?

I know we all try our best to manage everything on our hands and try to bring out the best in us. But while doing so, we engage in too many things and ultimately they take their toll.

It is becoming easier and easier every day where people have more work than ever on their hands. And their sole motive throughout life becomes, to find more and better ways of earning a better living. To find more things to be good and successful at.

We all have things on our hands to complete but let me tell you one thing. You won't be able to continue much longer if you keep with this burnout and exhaustion.

Our body is an engine and it needs a way of cooling down and tuning. So what's the first step you need to reduce burnout? You need to get the right amount of sleep.

There is this myth that you sleep one-third of your life so you don't need an 8-hour sleep. You can easily do the same with four hours and use the other four for more work. Trust me, this is not a myth, it is a misconception about proven research. Your body organs deserve at least half the time of what they spend serving us.

We can refresh and better our focus and cognitive skills once we have a good night's sleep full of dreams.

Another thing that most of us avoid doing is to say No to anyone anytime. The thing is that we don't have any obligation to anyone unless we are bound by a contract of blood or law to do or say anything that anyone tells us to do. The more we feel obligated to anyone, the more we try to do to impress that person or entity with our efforts and conduct.

This attitude isn't healthy for any relation. Excess of anything has never brought any good to anyone. So don't give up everything on just one thing. Instead, try to devise a balance between things. Over-commitment is never a good idea.

The third and final thing I want you to do is to give up on certain things at certain times. You don't need to carry your phone or laptop with you all day. This only creates a distraction even when you don't need to be in that environment.

You don't need to train your subconscious to be always alert on your emails and notifications or any incoming calls all day long. But sometimes you just need to give up on these things and zone out of your repetitive daily life.

Doing your best doesn't always mean giving yourself all out. Sometimes the best productive thing you can do is to relax. And that, my friends, can help you climb every mountain without ever getting tired of trying t do the same trail.

Chapter 23:

8 Ways On How To Start Taking Actions

Have you ever got caught up in situations when you can't bring yourself moving from deciding to doing? As a famous person once said, "Your beliefs become your thoughts; your thoughts become your words; your words become your actions; your actions become your habits; your habits become your values; your values become your destiny."

The first step towards success is by taking action. If you keep on thinking that you have to lose weight, start a business, learn a new language, or get another degree, you will end up nowhere without executing these thoughts into actions.

Here are 8 Ways To Start Moving The Needle In Your Life:

1. Decide that you want to get out of your comfort zone

The fear that we have that doesn't allow us to take action is that we might have to sacrifice our comfort zone in the process. And trust me, a lot of people aren't willing to do that. But if you don't step out of your comfort zone, how will you determine your true potential? You don't need the motivation to start taking action, and you just have to gather your willpower, stop with the excuses and procrastination, and get moving!

2. Don't indulge in the habit of Hesitatation

Have you had a great idea but then decide 10 minutes later that it was stupid. Ever wondered why that was? The answer is quite simple and straightforward; hesitation. We dwell on hesitation for too long. This makes it very difficult for us to get started on something. Thinking will only lead us to more and more thinking, which will lead us to a loop of continual thoughts, and our actions will get dominated by them. And then the regret that follows us is usually, "Why didn't we start earlier?" David Joseph Schwartz once said, "To fight fear, act. To increase fear – wait, put off, postpone."

3. Stop waiting for the perfect time:

There's a Chinese proverb that says, "The best time to plant a tree was 20 years ago. The second-best time is now." It means that there is no such thing as perfect timing. The minute we start to take action, the time becomes perfect. If we wait till everything gets in order or becomes exemplary, then we will be waiting forever. The ideal time in your eyes was last year, but the second-best time is right here and right now. It's never too late to start with your goals, dreams, and passions. All we have in our hands is the present time and what counts is how efficiently we spend this time. We must take action now and make adjustments along the way if we feel like it.

4. Don't pause and wait:

Have you ever found yourself thinking that, hey, it's a good day to wander around the city, but found yourself sitting and wasting time watching TV? Or you thought of doing your assignment but got caught up in a more hopeless task? Or you thought of presenting a new idea to your boss but got shied away? All of these thoughts, no matter how positive they were, stand nowhere unless you implement them. So stop being a talker and start being a doer. A doer is someone who immediately moves forward with his ideas. When we pause and look around, we will find ourselves making excuses and allow doubts to creep through into our minds. "The most difficult thing is the decision to act; the rest is merely tenacity." - Amelia Earhart.

5. Stop Over-thinking:

There's always an endless loop of overthinking that we can't get over with no matter how hard we try. From imagining the worst-case scenarios of even the best situations to getting anxious and depressed whenever any minor inconvenience happens, our mind tricks us into thinking that we can never get the best of both worlds (HM fans, I gotcha!) When we overthink stuff, we tend to get paralysis of analysis. We start to analyze every situation and obsess over how things aren't perfect, or the conditions aren't going our way. We question the amount of time that we have to commit and make endless excuses and reasons not to move forward with whatever we want to do.

6. Take continuous action:

The first step is the hardest step that we have to take. But once you get started, make sure that you fully commit yourself to your goal. Take continuous actions and keep up with your momentum by doing something related to your plan every day. Even if you are scheduling only 15-20 minutes of your life completing a small task, it will eventually add up into the more remarkable things. Moreover, it will help you build confidence by seeing your achievements. "It does not matter how slowly you go as long as you do not stop." - Confucius.

7. Overcome your fears:

We often succumb to our fears before even taking a step. The fear of failure, of not being good enough, of not doing enough, is the most common among them. Our mind tricks us into thinking that we might end up failing sooner or later. This prevents us from taking the first step and implementing our thoughts into actions. For example, suppose you're a professional speaker at a public speaking event. You have gained loads of experience, and you have no problem speaking to the lobby. But you do feel yourself getting nervous when you have to wait around for your turn. However, once you get started, all that fear and anxiety disappear. If you face similar situations in life, start being a doer, take action towards it and see how it will boost your confidence.

8. Eliminate any distractions:

We live in a world where distractions and procrastination have become more important than productivity. Have you ever found yourself thinking that you will take the online lecture for the subject you have been struggling with but ended up checking your social media accounts or watching irrelevant videos on YouTube? Procrastination is the primary reason we never end up doing what we should keep in our priorities. Instead, we should focus on our tasks, eliminate all the distractions and start with a slow but steady pace towards our goal. A single average idea put into action is far more valuable than those 20 genius ideas saved for another day or another time.

Conclusion:

Achieving your goals and dreams isn't an overnight task but takes years and decades to give you the final fruits. It's a road that will have setbacks, obstacles, lessons, and challenges. But what matters is that we shouldn't give up. We should face all the struggles and not surrender ourselves to our fears and demotivation. Converting your thoughts into actions and then enjoying the journey will equip you to thrive and see your goals become a reality in no time. So take into account what steps you took today. No matter how small they may be, appreciate and celebrate them.

Chapter 24:

Creating Successful Habits

Successful people have successful habits.

If you're stuck in life, feeling like you're not going anywhere, take a hard look at your habits.

Success is built from our small daily habits accumulated together,

Without these building blocks, you will not get far in life.

Precise time management, attention to detail, these are the traits of all who have made it big.

To change your life, you must literally change your life, the physical actions and the mindset.

Just as with success, the same goes with health.

Do you have the habit of a healthy diet and regular athletic exercises?

Healthy people have healthy habits.

If you are unhappy about your weight and figure, point the finger at your habits once again.

To become healthy, happy and wealthy, we must first become that person in the mind.

Success is all psychological.

Success has nothing to do with circumstances.

Until we have mastered the habits of our thinking we cannot project this success on the world.

We must first decide clearly who we want to be.

We must decide what our values are.

We must decide what we want to achieve.

Then we must discipline ourselves to take control of our destiny.

Once we know who we are and what we want to do,

Behaving as if it were reality becomes easy.

We must start acting the part.

That is the measure of true faith.

We must act as if we have already succeeded.

As the old saying goes: "fake it UNTIL YOU MAKE IT"

Commit yourself with unwavering faith.

Commit yourself with careful and calculated action.

You will learn the rest along the way

Every habit works towards your success or failure,

No matter how big or how small.

The more you change your approach as you fail, the better your odds
become.

Your future life will be the result of your actions today.

It will be positive or negative depending on your actions now.

You will attain free-will over your thoughts and actions.

The more you take control, the happier you will be.

Guard your mind from negativity.

Your mind is your sanctuary.

Ignore the scaremongering.

Treat your mind to pure motivation.

We cannot avoid problems.

Problems are a part of life.

Take control of the situation when it arises.

Have a habit of responding with action rather than fear.

Make a habit of noticing everybody and respecting everybody.

Build positive relationships and discover new ideas.

Be strong and courageous, yet gentle and reasonable.

These are the habits of successful leaders.

Be meticulous.

Be precise.

Be focused.

Make your bed in the morning.

Follow the path of drill sergeants in the royal marines and US navy seals.

Simple yet effective,

This one habit will shift your mindset first thing as you greet the new day.

Choose to meditate.

Find a comfortable place to get in touch with your inner-self.

Make it a habit to give yourself clarity of the mind and spirit.

Visualize your goals and make them a reality in your mind.

Choose to work in a state of flow.

Be full immersed in your work rather than be distracted.

To be productive we need to have an incredible habit of staying focused.

It will pay off.

It will pay dividends.

The results will be phenomenal.

Every single thing you choose to make a habit will add up.

No matter how big or how small,

Choose wisely.

Choose the habit of treating others with respect.

Treat the cleaner the same as you would with investors and directors.

Treat the poor the same as you would with the CEO of a multi-national company.

Our habits and attitude towards ourselves and others makes up our character.

Choose a habit of co-operation over competition,

After all the only true competition is with ourselves.

It doesn't matter whether someone is doing better than us as long as we are getting better.

If someone is doing better we should learn from them.

Make it a habit of putting ourselves into someone else's shoes.

We might stand to learn a thing or two.

No habit is too big or too small.

To be happy and successful we must do our best in them all.

Chapter 25:

<u>Believe in Yourself</u>

Listen up. I want to tell you a story. This story is about a boy. A boy who became a man, despite all odds. You see, when he was a child, he didn't have a lot going for him. The smallest and weakest in his class, he had to struggle every day just to keep up with his peers. Every minute of every hour was a fight against an opponent bigger and stronger than he was - and every day he was knocked down. Beaten. Defeated. But... despite that... despite everything that was going against him... this small, weak boy had one thing that separated him from hundreds of millions of people in this world. A differentiating factor that made a difference in the matter of what makes a winner in this world of losers. You see this boy believed in himself. No matter the odds, he believed fundamentally that he had the power to overcome anything that got in his way! It didn't matter how many times he was knocked down, he got RIGHT BACK UP!

Now it wasn't easy. It hurt like hell. Every time he failed was another reminder of how far behind he was. A reminder of the nearly insurmountable gap between him and everyone else and lurking behind that reminder was the temptation, the suggestion to just give up. Throw in the towel. Surrender the win. Yet believe me when I tell you that no matter HOW tough things got, no matter HOW much he wanted to give in, a small voice in his heart keep saying... not today... just once more... I know it hurts but I can try again... Just. Once. More.

You see more than anything in this world HE KNEW that deep inside him was a greatness just WAITING to be tapped into! A power that most people would never see, but not him. It didn't matter what the world threw at him, because he'd be damned if he let his potential die alongside him. And all it took? All it required to unlock the chasm of greatness inside was a moment to realise the lies the world tried to tell him. In less than a second he recognised the light inside that would ignite a spark of success to address the ones who didn't believe that he could do it. The ones who told him to give up! Get out! Go home and roam the streets where failure meets those who weren't born to sit at the seat at the top!

Yet what they didn't know is that being born weak didn't matter any longer 'cause in his fight to succeed he became stronger. Rising up to the heights beyond, he WOULD NOT GIVE UP till he forged a bond within his heart that ensured NO MATTER THE ODDS, no matter what anyone said about him, no matter what the world told him, he had something that NO ONE could take away from him. A power so strong it transformed this boy into a man. A loser into a winner. A failure into a success. That, is the power of self-belief...

Chapter 26:
Being 100% Happy Is Overrated

Lately I've been feeling as though happiness isn't something that truly lasts. Happiness isn't something that will stay with us very long. We may feel happy when we are hanging out with friends, but that feeling will eventually end once we part for the day. I've been feeling as though expecting to be constantly happy is very overrated. We try to chase this idea of being happy. We chase the material possessions, we chase the fancy cars, house, and whatever other stuff that we think will make us happy. But more often than not the desire is never really fulfilled. Instead, i believe that the feeling accomplishment is a much better state of mind to work towards. Things will never make us happy. We may enjoy the product we have worked so hard for temporarily. But that feeling soon goes away. And we are left wondering what is the next best thing we can aim our sights on. This never-ending chase becomes a repetitive cycle, one that we never truly are aware of but constantly desire. We fall into the trap that finding happiness is the end all-be-all.

What i've come to realise is that most of the time, we are actually operating on a more baseline level. A state that is skewed more towards the neutral end. Neither truly happy, or neither truly sad. And I believe that is perfectly okay. We should allow ourselves to embrace and accept the fact that it is okay to be just fine. Just neutral. Sure it isn't something very exciting, but we shouldn't put ourselves in a place where we expect to be constantly happy in order to lead a successful life. This revelation came when I realised that every time I felt happy, I would experience a crash in mood the next day. I would start looking at instagram, checking up on my friends, comparing their days, and thinking that they are leading a happier life than I was. I would then start berating myself and find ways to re-create those happy moments just for the sake of it. Just because I thought i needed to feel happy all the time. It was only when I actually sat down and started looking inwards did I realise that maybe I can never truly find happiness from external sources.

Instead of trying to find happiness in things and external factors that are beyond my control, I started looking for happiness from within myself. I began to appreciate how happy I was simply being alone. Being by myself. Not letting other factors pull me down. I found that I was actually happiest when I was taking a long shower, listening to my own thoughts. No music playing, no talking to people, just me typing away on my computer, writing down all the feelings I am feeling, all the thoughts that I am thinking, letting every emotion I was feeling out of my system. I started to realise that the lack of distractions, noise, comparisons with others, free from social media, actually provided me with a clearer mind. It was in those brief moments where I found myself to be my most productive, with ideas streaming all over the place. It was in that state of mind that I did feel somewhat happy. That I could create that state of mind without depending on other people to fulfil it for me.

If any of you out there feel that your emotions are all over the place, maybe it is time for you to sit down by yourself for a little while. Stop searching for happiness in things and stuff, and sometimes even people. We think it is another person's job to make us happy. We expect to receive compliments, flowers, a kiss, in order to feel happy. While those things are certainly nice to have, being able to find happiness from within is much better. By sitting and reflecting in a quiet space, free from any noise and distractions, we may soon realise that maybe we are okay being just okay. Maybe we don't need expensive jewellery or handbags or fancy houses to make us happy. Maybe we just need a quiet mind and a grateful spirit.

The goal is to find inner peace. To accept life for the way it is. To accept things as the way they are. To be grateful for the things we have. That is what it means to be happy.

Chapter 27:

7 Reasons Your Beliefs Are Holding You Back

You know that you have immense potential in your heart, and you are also working hard to attain your desired results, but something still doesn't fit right. Your beliefs might be consciously or unconsciously sabotaging your potential through your actions. This might create the less-than-desirable results that are holding you back from your real success.

Here are some 5 beliefs that might be getting in your way. Observe and analyze them, and start getting rid of them so that your path to success becomes easy and thorn-free.

C

1. Beliefs Are More Powerful Than You Think

"Beliefs have the power to create and the power to destroy. Human beings have the awesome ability to take any experience of their lives and create a meaning that disempowers them or one that can literally save their lives." - Tony Robbins. To change our lives, we first have to change our mindset and what we believe in so dearly. Challenging your beliefs is the key element to improve yourself. If we look around us, we might find a few limiting beliefs in the blink of an eye.

2. Everyone will get ahead of me if I rest.

This is perhaps the most crucial limiting belief that the majority of people go through. Many of us think that if we take some time off for ourselves, we'll fall behind in life, and everyone will get ahead of us, crushing us beneath them. For this particular reason, we stop focusing on our needs and necessities and burns out all of our energy on things that should come as second on our lists. Instead, we should convert our "shoulds" into "musts" and focus on ourselves too. Meditating for an hour, going to the gym, taking some time off for hanging out with friends or watching a movie alone, reading a book that's not connected to your work, these all are necessary to sustain life. Making excuses for not taking any time off for yourself and working day and night tirelessly will drain your energy or become a problem for your health; likewise, you will be tired physically and mentally and wouldn't be able to do your tasks on time.

3. Everyone is succeeding in life but me.

With the increasing social media norms and the lives of celebrities on every cover page, or seeing everyone around you figuring their lives out and enjoying themselves, you might feel that you are the only one who hasn't got a thing right. Unfortunately, human nature shows the world our successes and happiness rather than telling them our weak, struggling phases and vulnerability. Comparing yourself to those around you or any celebrity or influencer from social media may become a downward spiral for you when you are feeling confused and lost. Believing that everyone has it easy and you are the only one struggling could make you feel demotivated and depressed. This would, in turn, make you lazy, and you would eventually stop working towards your goal and passion.

4. I can never be good enough.

This limiting belief is the most common one among the people. Initially, they would give their all to a new job, a new relationship, or a new task. Then, if things wouldn't work out for them, they would just blame their performance and themselves and would label it as "I'm not good enough for this." This often leads to being anxious and finding perfection in things. And if failed to achieve this, one starts to procrastinate, thinking that their energies and efforts will eventually go to waste anyway. The little voice inside your head telling you that you're not good enough might also make you believe that you're not skilled enough or talented enough for the job or not deserving enough to be with the person you like. As a result, you pull yourself back and miss out on any opportunities offered to you.

5. I am capable enough to do everything myself.

We're often fooled by the idea that we don't need anyone's help, and we can figure out everything independently. This approach is majorly toxic as we all need a helping hand now and then. No one walks on the path of success alone. You may feel ashamed or guilty in asking for help or may think that you will be rejected or let down, or may think of yourself as the superior creature who knows everything and are not ready to listen to anyone else. All this might bring you down at one point in your life. We should always be open to any criticism and feedback and should never shy away from asking any help or advice from the people we trust and from the people we get inspired from.

6. The tiny voice becomes too loud sometimes

Limiting beliefs does impede us in some way. There's always this tiny voice in the back of our heads that keeps whispering thoughts and ideas into our minds. Most of what the voice tells us are negative stuff, and the worst part is that we actually start to believe in all of that. "You can never lose weight; stop trying. You're unattractive, and you won't find your significant other any time soon. You don't have the mindset or money to start up your own business; get yourself a 9-5 job instead." All of these, and much more, are what pulls us back from the things that we want to say or the stuff that we want to do.

7. The time isn't right.

The time isn't right, and believe me, it never will be. You're wasting your life away thinking that you will get married, lose your weight, learn a new skill, start your own business, all when the time will be correct. But there's no such as the right time. You either start doing what you want or sit on the side-lines and watch someone else do it. The right time is here and now. It would be best if you started doing the things you want until you make up your mind that you want to do it. You don't have to wait for a considerable amount of money to start a business; start with a small one instead. You don't have to settle down first to get married; find someone who will grow with you and help you. You don't need to spend hours and hours in the gym to lose weight; start eating healthy. There is no right time for anything, but the time becomes right when you decide to change yourself and your life for the better.

Conclusion:

You can make a thousand excuses or find a million experiences to back up your beliefs, but truth be told, you should always be aware of the assumptions you are creating and how they may be affecting your life. For example, will your beliefs stop you from taking action towards your life? Or will you change them into new and creative opportunities to get the results you want?

Chapter 28:

Dealing With Difficult People

It is inevitable that people will rub us the wrong way as we go about our days. Dealing with such people requires a lot of patience and self-control, especially if they are persistent in their actions towards you over a lengthy period of time.

Difficult people are outside the realm of our control and hence we need to implement strategies to deal with negative emotions should they arise. If you encounter such people frequently, here are 7 ways that you can take back control of the situation.

1.   Write Your Feelings Down Immediately
A lot of times we bottle up feelings when someone is rude or unpleasant to us. We may have an urge to respond but in the moment we choose not to. In those circumstances, the next best thing we can do is to write down our feelings either in our journals or in our smartphones as notes.

Writing our feelings down is a therapeutic way to cleanse our thoughts and negative energy. In writing we can say the things we wished we had said, and find out the reasons that made us feel uneasy in the first place. In writing we are also able to clearly identify the trigger points and could work backwards in managing our expectations and feelings around the person. If it is a rude customer, or a rude stranger, we may not be able to respond for fear or retaliation or for fear of losing our jobs. It is best those situations not to erupt in anger, but take the time to work through those emotions in writing.

2.   Tell The Person Directly What You Dislike About Their Attitude

If customer service and retail isn't your profession, or if it is not your boss, you may have the power to voice your opinion directly to the person who wronged you. If confrontation is something that you are comfortable with, don't hesitate to express to them why you are dissatisfied with their treatment or attitude towards you. You may also prefer to clear your head before coming back to confront the person and not let emotions escalate. A fight is the last thing we want out of this communication.

3.   Give An Honest Feedback Where Possible On Their Website

If physical confrontation is not your cup of tea, consider writing in a feedback online to express your dissatisfaction. We are usually able to write the most clear and precise account of the situation when we have time to process what went wrong. Instead of handling this confrontation ourselves, the Human Resources team would most likely deal with this person directly, saving you the trouble in the process. Make sure to give an accurate account of the situation and not exaggerate the contents to make the person look extremely in the wrong, although it can be tough to contain our emotions when we are so riled up.

4. Use this Energy To Fuel Your Fire

Sometimes, taking all these energy and intense emotions we feel may fuel our fire to work harder or to prove to others that we are not deserving of their hatred. Be careful though not to take things too far. Remember that ultimately you have the power to choose whether to let this person affect you. If you choose to accept these emotions, use them wisely.

5. Channel This Intense Emotion Into A Craft That Allows You To Release Unwanted Feelings

For those who have musical talents, we may use this negative experience to write a song about it while we are at the heights of our emotions. In those moments the feelings are usually intense, and we all know that emotions can sometimes produce the best works of art. If playing an instrument, writing an article, producing a movie clip, or crushing a sport is something that comes natural to us, we may channel and convert these emotions into masterpieces. Think Adele, Taylor Swift, and all the great songwriters of our generation as an example.

6. Learn To Grow Your Patience

Sometimes not saying anything at all could be the best course of action. Depending on the type of person you are, and the level of zen you have in you, you may not be so easily phased by negativity if you have very high control of your emotions. Through regular meditation and deep breathing, we can let go of these bad vibes that people send our way and just watch it vanish into a cloud of smoke. Regular yoga and meditation practices are good ways to train and grow your patience.

7.   Stand Up For Yourself

At the end of the day, you have to choose when and if you want to stand up for yourself if someone has truly wronged you. We can only be so patient and kind to someone before we snap. Never be afraid to speak your truth and defend yourself if you feel that you have been wrongfully judged. Difficult people make our lives unpleasant but it doesn't mean we should allow them to walk all over us without consequences. You have every right to fight for your rights, even if it means giving up something important in the process to defend it.

Chapter 29:

10 Habits of Shawn Mendes

Shawn Peter Raul Mendes was born on 8th August 1998 in Toronto, Canada. The music superstar has rocked the industry with his talent which until 2013 was barely known.

These are ten habits of Shawn Mendes:

1. He Is Social

Shawn rose to fame in 2013 after posting his video cover of Justin Bieber's *as long as you love me* to his Vine social account. The six-second video spread like wildfire on the internet and netizens wanted to know more about the then 15-year-old teenager.

He currently has over 28 million YouTube subscribers and 64 million Instagram followers with whom he shares his life and work. He is outgoing and very interactive with his fans in his tours and live performances.

2. He Is A Fast Learner

Shawn Mendes is the embodiment of fast learning. His ability to comprehend and grasp skills faster than a majority of people is unmatched. Did you know that he learned how to play the guitar through YouTube?

In his interview with Spotify, he revealed that his father challenged him that he would get Shawn a guitar if he learned to play using a rented one for a couple of weeks. He accepted the challenge and started tutorials on YouTube.

3. He Is Hardworking

Shawn is a hardworking musician. Hitherto, he has released two live albums, four studio albums, twenty music videos, and three extended plays. All this has been accomplished within the short time he has been doing music.

Moreover, despite his rise to fame while still learning, Shawn has managed to juggle between music and academics successfully. He went for his world tour to further his music but still took online classes and managed to graduate with his class in 2016.

4. He Is Collaborative

Shawn is a rising superstar in music and he has featured other music giants in his songs. He has featured Camila Cabello on various tracks including *I know what you did last summer* and *Senorita* both of which have won several awards.

Other singers that have partnered with Shawn are Justin Bieber in *Monster,* Julia Michaels in *Like to be you,* and Khalid in *Youth.* He is open to more collaborations with other artists because he does not see them as a threat to his fan base.

5. <u>He Is Bold</u>

Shawn has been subject to many rumors since he came to the limelight. It was once rumored that he is gay and later also rumored that he had an affair with Taylor Swift and Camila Cabello. At all times, Shaw has maintained a straight face and such rumors have never made him shy away from music.

He once got a chance to clear the air when hosted by Dax Shepard in his podcast. He explained that he is not gay although he had close friends who were. It could be what contributed to the spreading of the rumors.

6. <u>He Is Ambitious</u>

Shawn is an ambitious young man pursuing his music career to the best he can make out of it. He has worked on several projects simultaneously as he completed his high school education. Nothing has obstructed his sight from pursuing his dreams.

He has done four world tours to promote his music and is looking forward to the wonder world tour from March 2022.

7. <u>He Is Visionary</u>

Shawn is a visionary young man. He has not forgotten his vision despite amassing wealth and fame. He launched the Shawn Mendes Foundation on 28th August 2019. This is a rare action by young celebrities worldwide.

The foundation seeks to empower youth change makers, their organizations, and their work. As Shawn reminisces about his journey to starting music, he envisions an empowered society.

8. <u>He Does Charity Work</u>

Shawn has developed the habit of doing charity. Both through his foundation and other channels, Shawn has heavily given back to the community.

Some of the causes he has supported are disaster relief, education, abuse, grief support, homelessness, health, and senior citizen support.

9. <u>He Loves Playing The Guitar</u>

Shawn loves playing strings before he perfected his skill from YouTube video tutorials. From his teenage years, he has always moved with his guitar in every concert he performs.

He learned to play the guitar since he was 13 years and it has been his signature musical instrument despite him being able to hire instrumentalists.

10.<u>He Is Creative</u>

Shawn is a creative person. He has written hit songs one after another. This is growth from when he used to sing covers of other artists' songs. His creativity has expanded evident in how he connects with his fans through his songs.

In conclusion, these ten habits of Shawn Mendes are part of his lifestyle; some of which are hidden from the public.

Chapter 30:

When It Is Time To Let Go and Move On (Career)

Today we're going to talk about a topic that I hope will motivate you to quit that job that you hate or one that you feel that you have nothing more to give anymore.

For the purpose of this video, we will focus mainly on career as I believe many of you may feel as though you are stuck in your job but fear quitting because you are afraid you might not find a better one.

For today's topic, I want to draw attention to a close friend of mine who have had this dilemma for years and still hasn't decided to quit because he is afraid that he might not get hired by someone else.

In the beginning of my friend's career, he was full of excitement in his new job and wanted to do things perfectly. Things went pretty smoothly over the course of the first 2 years, learning new things, meeting new friends, and getting settled into his job that he thought he might stay on for a long time to come seeing that it was the degree that he had pursued in university. However when the 3rd year came along, he started to feel jaded with his job. Everyday he would meet ungrateful and sometimes mean customers who were incredibly self-entitled. They would be rude and he started dreading going to work more and more each day. This aspect of the job wore him down and he started to realise that he wasn't happy at all with his work.

Having had a passion for fitness for a while now, he realized that he felt very alive when he attended fitness classes and enjoyed working out and teaching others how to work out. He would fiddle with the idea of attending a teacher training course that would allow him to be a professional and certified fitness coach.

As his full time job started to become more of a burden, he became more serious about the prospect of switching careers and pursuing a new one entirely. At his job, realized that the company wasn't generous at all with the incentives and gruelling work hours, but he stayed on as he was afraid he wouldn't find another job in this bad economy. The fear was indeed real so he kept delaying trying to quit his job. Before he knew it 3 years more had passed and by this time he full on dreaded every single minute at his job.

It was not until he made that faithful decision one day to send in his resignation letter and to simultaneously pay for the teacher training course to become a fitness instructor did his fortunes start to change for him. The fortunes in this wasn't about money. It was about freedom. It was about growth. And it was about living.

We all know deep in our hearts when it is time to call it quits to something. When we know that there is nothing more that we can possibly give to our job. That no amount of time more could ever fulfill that void in us. That we just simply need to get out and do something different.

You see, life is about change. As we grow, our priorities change, our personalities change, our expectations change, and our passions and our interests change as well. If we stay in one place too long, especially in a field or in something that we have hit a wall at, we will feel stuck, and we will feel dread. We will feel that our time spent is not productive and we end up feeling hopeless and sorry for ourselves.

Instead when we choose to let go, when we choose to call time on something, we open up the doors for time on other ventures, and other adventures. And our world becomes brighter again.

I challenge each and everyone of you to take a leap of faith. You know deep in your hearts when it is time to move on from your current job and find the next thing. If you dont feel like you are growing, or if you feel that you absolutely hate your job because there is no ounce of joy that you can derive from it, move on immediately. Life is too short to be spending 10 hours of your life a day on something that you hate, that sucks the living soul out of you. Give yourself the time and space to explore, to find some other path for you to take. You will be surprised what might happen when you follow your heart.

Chapter 31:

6 Ways To Get People To Like You

We are always trying for people to like us. We work on ourselves so that we can impress them. Everyone can not enjoy a single person. There will always be someone who dislikes them. But, that one person does not stop us from being charming and making people like us. In today's generation, good people are difficult to find. We all have our definition of being liked. We all have our type of person to select. That makes it very hard for someone to like someone by just knowing their name. We always judge people quickly, even to understand their nature. That makes it hard to like someone.

People always work their selves to be liked by the majority of people. It gives you a sense of comfort knowing that people are happy with you. You feel at ease when you know that people around you tend to smile by thinking about you. For that, you need to make an excellent first impression on people. Training yourself in such a way that you become everyone's favorite can sure be tiring. But, it always comes with a plus point.

1. **Don't Judge**

If you want people to like you, then you need to stop judging them. It is not good to consider someone based on rumors or by listening to one side of the story. Don't judge at all. We can never have an idea of what's going on in an individual life. We can not know what they are going through without them telling us. The best we can do is not judge them. Give them time to open up. Let them speak with you without the fear of being judged. Assuming someone is the worst without you them knowing is a horrendous thing to do.

2. Let Go of Your Ego and Arrogance

Make people feel like they can talk to you anytime they want. Arrogance will lead you nowhere. You will only be left alone in the end. So, make friends. Don't be picky about people. Try to get to know everyone with their own stories and theories. Make them feel comfortable around you to willingly come to talk to you and feel at ease after a few words with you. Being egotistic may make people fear you, but it will not make people like you. Be friendly with everyone around you.

3. Show Your Interest In People

When people talk about their lives, let them. Be interested in their lives, so it will make them feel unique around you. Make sure you listen attentively to their rant and remember as much as possible about a person. Even if they talk about something boring, try to make an effort towards them. If they talk about something worth knowledge, appreciate them. Ask them questions about it, or share your part of information with them, if you have any on that subject. Just try to make an effort, and people will like you instantly.

4. Try To Make New Friends

People admire others when they can click with anyone they meet. Making new friends can be a challenge, but it gives you confidence and, of course, new friends. Try to provide an excellent first impression and show them your best traits. Try to be yourself as much as possible, but do not go deep into friendship instantly. Give them time to adapt to your presence. You will notice that they will come to you themselves. That is because they like being around you. They trust you with their time, and you should valve it.

5. Be Positive

Everyone loves people. You give a bright, positive vibe. They tend to go to them, talk to them and listen to them. People who provide positive energy are easy to communicate with, and we can almost instantly become friends. Those are the type of people we can trust and enjoy being around. Positivity plays a critical role in your want to be liked. It may not be easy, but practice makes perfect. You have to give it your all and make everyone happy.

6. Be Physically and Mentally Present For The People Who Need You

People sometimes need support from their most trusted companion. You have to make sure you are there for them whenever they need you. Be there for them physically, and you can comfort someone without even speaking with them. Just hug them or just try to be there for them. It will make them feel peaceful by your presence. Or be there emotionally if they are ready. Try to talk to them. Listen to whatever they have to say, even if it doesn't make sense. And if they need comfort. Try to motivate them with your words.

Conclusion

You need to improve yourself immensely if you want people to like you. Make sure you do the right thing at the right time. Make people trust you and make them believe your words. Even a small gesture can make people like you. Have the courage to change yourself so that people will like you with all their heart's content.

Chapter 32:

Share Your Troubles Freely and Openly

Life is hard. We go through tons of challenges, problems, and obstacles every single day. We accumulate problems and stresses left right and Center. Absorbing each impact blow for blow.

Over time, these impacts will wear us down mentally and physically. Without a proper release channel, we find that our emotions spill over in ways when we least expect it. We get easily irritated, have a hard time falling asleep, have mood issues, and find ourselves even being temporarily depressed at times.

When we bottle negativity, it festers inside us without us realising what we have done. That is where releasing those tensions by pouring our heart and soul into friends, writing, journaling, and other outlets that allow us to express our feelings freely without judgement.

We may not all have friends that we can truly count on to share our deepest darkest secrets for fear that they might share these secrets unsuspectingly. If we do have these types of friends, treasure them and seek them out regularly to share your problems. By bouncing ideas off someone, we may even find a new solution to an old problem that we couldn't before. The other party may also be able to see things more objectively and with a unique perspective that is contrary to yours which you could potentially use to your advantage.

If writing things down is something that helps you cope with life, then by all means take a piece of paper and write down all the things that have been bothering you. Journal it, archive it. You may even write a song about it if that helps you process things better. Writing things down help us clear our minds and lets us see the big picture when we come back to it at a later date should we feel ready to address it. When things are too crazy, we may not have the mental capacity to handle everything being thrown at us at one go. So take the time to sort those feelings out.

You may also choose to just find a place that brings you relaxation. Whether it be going to the beach, or renting a hotel, or even just screaming at the top of your lungs. Let those feelings out. Don't keep it hidden inside.

IF all these things still don't work for you, you may want to try seeking help from a professional counsellor or therapist who can work out these issues you have in your life one by one. Never be afraid to book an appointment because your mental health is more important than the stigma associated with seeing a professional. You are not admitting you have a problem, you are simply acknowledge that there are areas in your life that you need assistance with. And that it is perfectly okay and perfectly normal to do so. Counsellors have the passion to serve, the passion to help, and that is why they chose that profession to being with. So seek their assistance and guidance as much as you need to.

Life isn't easy. But we can all take a conscious effort to regulate our emotions more healthily to live a long and balanced life.

Chapter 33:

Playing To Your Strengths

Have you ever asked yourself why you fail at everything you touch?

Why you seem to lack behind everyone you strive to beat?

Why you can't give up the things that are keeping you from achieving the goals you dream?

Has anyone told you the reason for all this?

You might wonder about it all your life and might never get to the right answer. Even though you stare at the answer every day in the mirror.

Yes! It's you! You are the reason for your failures.

You are the reason for everything bad going on in your life right now.

But you are also the master of your life, and you should start acting like one.

When the world brings you down, find another way to overcome the pressures.

Find another way to beat the odds.

Adverse situations only serve to challenge you.

Be mentally strong and bring the world to your own game.

Show the world what you are.

Show the world what you are capable of.

Don't let anyone dictate to you what you should do.

Rather shape your life to dictate the outcome with your efforts and skills.

You can't always be wrong.

Somewhere, and somehow, you will get the right answer.

That will be your moment to build what you lost.

That will be your moment to shut everyone else and rise high in the silence of your opponents.

If you don't get that chance, don't wait for it to come.

Keep going your way and keep doing the things you do best.

Paths will open to your efforts one day.

You can't be bad at everything you do.

You must be good at something.

Find out what works for you.

Find out what drives your spirit.

Find out what you can do naturally while being blind-folded with your hands tied behind your back.

There is something out there that is calling out to you.

Once you find it, be the best at it as you can.

It doesn't matter if you do not get to the top.

You don't anything to prove to anyone.

You only need one glimpse of positivity to show yourself that you have something worthwhile to live for.

Always challenge yourself.

If you did 5 hours of work today, do 7 tomorrow.

If you run 1 mile today, hit 3 by the end of the week.

You know exactly what you are capable of.

Play to your strengths.

Make it your motto to keep going every single day.

Make a decision.

Be decisive.

Stick with it.

Don't be afraid because there is nothing to fear.

The only thing to fear is the fear itself.

Tell your heart and your mind today, that you can't stop, and you won't stop.

Till the time you have the last breath in your lungs and the last beat in your heart, keep going.

You will need to put your heart out to every chance you can get to raise yourself from all this world and be invincible.

You have no other option but to keep going.

To keep trying until you have broken all the barriers to freedom.

You are unique and you know it.

You just need to have the guts to admit that you are special and live up to the person you were always meant to be.

Take stock of yourself today.

Where are you right now and where do you want to be?

The moment you realize your true goal, that is the moment you have unlocked your strengths.

Live your life on your terms.

Every dream that you dream is obtainable.

And the only way is to believe in yourself.

To believe that you are the only thing standing in the way of your past and your future.

Once you have started, tell yourself that there is no return.

Dictate your body to give up only when you have crossed the finish line.

Start acting on every whim that might get you to the ultimate fate.

These whims are your strength because you have them for a purpose.

Why walk when you can run?

Why run when you can fly?

Why listen when you can sing?

Why go out and dine when you can cook?

The biggest gift that you can give to yourself is the mental satisfaction that you provide yourself.

You are only limited to the extent you cage yourself.

The time you let go will be your salvation. But you have to let go!

Chapter 34:
Happy People Create Time to Do What They Love Every Day

Most of our days are filled with things that we need to do and the things we do to destress ourselves. But, in between all this, we never get time for things. We wanted to do things that bring us pure joy. So then the question is, When will we find time to do what we love? Then, when things calm down a bit and when the people who visit us leave or finish all the trips we have planned and wrap up our busy projects, and the kids will be grown, we will retire? Then, probably after we are dead, we will have more time.

You do not have to wait for things to get less busy or calmer. There will always be something coming up; trips, chores, visitors, errands, holidays, projects, death and illness. There is never going to be more time. Whatever you have been stuck in the past few years, it will always be like that. So now the challenge is not waiting for things to change it is to make time for things you love no matter how busy your life is. Sit down and think about what you want to do, something that you have been putting off. What is something that makes you feel fulfilled and happy? Everyone has those few things that make them fall in love with life think of what is that for you. If you haven't figured it out yet, we will give you some examples, and maybe you can try some of these things and see how that makes you feel.

- Communing with nature

- Going for a beautiful walk

- Creating or growing a business or an organization

- Hiking, running, biking, rowing, climbing

- Meditating, journaling, doing yoga, reflecting

- Communing with loved ones

- Crafting, hogging, blogging, logging, vlogging
- Reading aloud to kids
- Reading aloud to kids

Did you remember something you enjoyed doing, but as the responsibilities kept increasing, you sidelined it. Well, this is your sign to start doing what you loved to take time out for that activity every day, even if it is for 30 minutes only. Carve that time out for yourself, do it now. Once you start doing this, you will realize that you will have more energy because your brain will release serotonin, and your energy level will increase. Secondly, your confidence will improve because you will be making something love every day, and that will constantly help you gain confidence because you will be putting yourself in a happy, self-loving state. You will notice that you have started enjoying life more when you do something you love once a day. It makes the rest of your day brighter and happier. You will also want to constantly continue learning and growing because your brain will strive to do more and more of the thing you like to do, and that will eventually lead to an increased desire of learning and growing. Lastly, your motivation will soar because you will have something to look forward to that brings you pure joy.

CPSIA information can be obtained
at www.ICGtesting.com
Printed in the USA
LVHW081959130122
708314LV00013B/578